Anatomy of a Dress

by

Juliette van der Molen

First published 2019 by The Hedgehog Poetry Press

Published in the UK by
The Hedgehog Poetry Press
5 Coppack House
Churchill Avenue
Clevedon
BS21 6QW

www.hedgehogpress.co.uk

ISBN: 978-1-9160908-9-7

9 8 7 6 5 4 3 2 1

A CIP Catalogue record for this book is available from the British
Library.

For my darling daughter Chloe, a dress designer in her own right, who through her fierce independence and confidence taught me the value in being myself no matter what I am wearing.

Also by Juliette van der Molen:

Death Library: The Exquisite Corpse Collection

Mother, May I?

'Anatomy of A Dress' explores messages regarding how women have historically been encouraged to dress, mainly for the pleasure and subjugation of the patriarchy. Poems for this book were written as the final culmination of thoughts and research that developed over a couple of years. This process began with a visit to the Metropolitan Museum of Art in New York City. I was not writing poetry at that time. Focused on visual art, I stumbled upon an exhibit of Charles James' gowns at the Met Costume Institute. This exhibit inspired sketches and abstract paintings. I spent hours sketching his specific architecture and people watching as visitors viewed the exhibit. I began to research James and other designers within the context of his times. While viewing the Catwalk Rijksmuseum exhibit in Amsterdam, I began to consider the changes in fashion and how they seemed based on whatever the current definition of women's roles were at the time. The evolution from Charles James' structural gowns to Yves Saint Laurent's female tuxedo is an echo of social change for women underneath the patriarchal rule.

When I began the poems for this book my thoughts took a personal turn. I began to think about ideas I had been brought up to believe about how people dress and what it says about them. I started to realize that many of my memories were loaded with markers about what I was wearing at a specific point in time. As a woman who was taught to enjoy shopping and dressing at a young age, I have a love/hate relationship with clothing. These conflicts and memories are folded into the poetry of this book. I realized that sometimes encouragements or rules were handed down to me by those of my own gender, from grandmother to mother. It has made me aware of how much women can participate in perpetuating the oppression of the patriarchy without overt intent. These reinforcements by my own gender support a male led society that has a vested interest in the disenfranchisement of women.

This poetry speaks about my struggle and the difficulties that some women face when making a decision that most men would consider simple—

What should I wear today?

Contents

MY HEM

my hem is not
the waterline
of marked desire
or intention
it is just
a finished
edge that falls
here
or
there.
it is not
a signal
to send hands
into a
traffic pattern
or to
obstruct.
it is not up
for debate
or
for speculation,
it asks
for nothing.

ZIP ME

turn around
and let me
zip you,
he says.

teeth meshed
neat, slide
against my
slip.

they used to
call me, a
slip—
of a thing,
not anymore.

closed in,
whispered
up a back,
vertebrae track,
curved to spine.

all done,
perfect—
he says,
satisfied.

molded plastic
coils, holding in—
all my
secrets,
stowed underneath.

until i let
them out,
all alone,
twisting—
contorted arms
and spine,
slider drawn
against
slip.

you zip me in,
now
i zip me out,
i am finally—
perfect.

BUTTONED UP

button your lip
in addition to
the dress.
slipped straight
and tight,
center line from
sacrum to neck,
a white spine
on top of spine.
something old—
this expectation
of choked roses,
an aisle—
dead girl walking.
something blue—
swollen lips
of baby's breath
that never dies,
but only he
can reach the
buttons,
fingers fumble,
twist and pull
until the fabric
fitted on to you,
sewn into
the architecture
of a virgin bride—
rips, the sound of
lace shredding sets
your teeth on edge,
and still you say
nothing, when he pushes
you to the floor
in favor of buttons
he can handle,
this man you used to adore.

DART

steamed edge
folded tight along
a seam that kisses
underneath my arm
to perky apex,
two of them,
cupped over me
where you think
your hands
should be—
instead your eyes
travel the line
that defines me
darted to a bullseye
this game you play
that makes me
wish for flour sacks,
shapeless,
made for hiding—
except that's not me.

WON'T YOU CALL ME SWEETHEART?

seeded pearls perch
along the edge
of these curves,
hiding my skin
with the idea
of a heart,
a stylized perfection,
unbreakable,
unwinnable— too.
dipped deep,
hugged tight,
flesh lifted in offering
that isn't enough
for fingers that
squeezed inside,
gripping my curves
to pull and shred,
tears tumbling from
my eyes, fallen
among these
seeds of yesterday,
while you mumble
'sweetheart', slipped against
this neckline—
it's not your fault,
this pillage,
this rummage,
uncontrollable,
i should know better
than to drive you wild.

SILHOUETTE SHAME

bedrock formation,
but from a fissure—
grown,
bloomed,
beneath careful hands
and watchful gaze,
dressed up in
Cinderella silhouettes
and mother's high heels,
that always felt
too big— to fill,
until they weren't.
a tide pulls—
swelled to bleeding,
a body curved
with hips meant
to hold and cradle—
beyond play-acting,
eyes of a child,
body of a woman—
zipped,
into sheaths
with hems to tempt
eyes and fingers,
a primal prowl
in backseats
under cover of darkness.
my mouth open,
resistance swallowed,
hands mold me
into shame
as the moon bobs
through a car window,
and the swings on
the playground are stilled
beneath an eyeful sky.

SCHOOLED PLEATS

goodbye gathered waists
with grosgrain ribbon
tied neat by someone
else's hands,
these hand—
my own,
stitch sharp knife pleats,
sliced through painful
adolescence—
a departure from
innocence and faith
in parental devotion.

a midriff exposed,
belly soft,
sucked in tight
by bulimic conversation
between classes,
hovered over porcelain
spilling secrets that
contaminate my insides,
acrid acid against teeth—
wet eyes that shine
underneath a raised hand.

straight A's at the top
of your class,
knee socks cling
to calves you'll touch
when you tell me
how sorry you are,
about my broken home—
desire masqueraded
as concern, while you
open me and fill me
with all the things i
need to purge.

DUPIONI DARKLING

draped stiff and thick
enough to hold
shape whether i
am inside or out,
dupioni constructed
cage, legs inside a
bell held together,
my voice clangs
while he,
shakes
-and-
turns
me upside down
until the world
tumbles,
hands cemented
to waist,
ankle bone soldered
to ankle bone,
a skirt shaded over
eyes while fingers
prise the length
of calves,
jaws of life
at fragile knees
but all i see
in the dark is
the silk
and
over-bloomed
petals.

S(MOCKED)

puckered tight,
disapproving lips,
where threads have
pulled and gathered
red and white gingham
checks across a chest
that doesn't know how
to expand, just yet.
tennis shoes tied
in double knots,
sun licking pavement
until it is gooey,
spongy with heat.
i pull at cotton filled
elastic, a sticky hug
clinging without consent
ruffled straps slipped off shoulders
until i am free,
like my brother,
my cousin—
who bare their chests
in blazing June heat.
shock and awe
at my newfound
bravery, which
isn't bravery at all,
but a misunderstanding
of the rules, of what
girls don't do.

the edge of my bobbed
hair cutting a knife-line
into my cheeks,
while my head hangs
and mother covers me,
but not before a picture
that everyone will laugh
at for years to come:
wasn't she cute when
she didn't understand?
when she thought she
could do anything,
just like the boys?

EYE LET

i let breath in,
arms raised
for a torso
wrapped
in whalebone stays—
cords,
ribbons,
thongs and things.

swooped swift laces
through eyelets
until i am
a puppet of flesh
squeezed in from the
middle—
to perfection.

brought in,
by degrees,
so much better if only
my rib cage
weren't in the way.

internal organs
squish
&
sway
until my heart feels
like it is
lodged at the base
of my throat
and my insides
ache, pulled too
fast, too tight—
you couldn't wait.

but this hourglass
runs out of sand
more quickly than
we think,
& i let
your eyes devour
what's left
which is not much
when i am reduced
to silk & stays.

PRÊT-À-PORTER

chosen for me
always blue
never red,
that was for other
girls,
— blue —
like your eyes
she said, keep
them looking up
into your face,
a whispered secret—
we are on the same side.

lace collars,
peter pan starches,
a pearl button
slipped through elastic
neatly tucking me away
again. don't pull,
she said,
no tugging—
good girls don't fidget.

until the mall,
and
car keys,
sweet freedom
in circular racks,
hard rock music,
a fistful of green
still wadded in my
pocket, first job—
sixteen.

skirts to hide,
shoved in backpacks
changed between the
clang of lockers
and savior bells.
quick spin dial—
second wardrobe stashed,
the one that belongs
to that
'good girl'.

books dropped,
subversive upskirts
and sly smiles
sharing secrets
i didn't know
how to tell.
a man i call Mr.—
grade book in hand,
hot breath on my neck
marking me absent,
making me sick.

tugs at sleeves,
belly sucked in—
or thighs that swim
beneath denim
made for a mannequin.
never quite right,
me—
not the dress,
proportions judged
in silence, until i
confess my sins
to a porcelain saint
that flushes me clean.

couture beyond reach
as i stand
arms outstretched
from the center line—
in this flyover state,
fingers stretched,
looking for a land
without bargain bins
or second hand stores,
in my prêt-à-porter
craving distant shores.

GIRLS ON PARADE

flown high,
small voices
turned loud
for crowds,
synchronized—
to one breath.

hair pulled tight
bound and topped
in glitter gleaming
below lights,
lifting spirits
for jerseys and
pads and helmets
on a Friday Night.

a v-notch,
modern,
spankies printed
to draw the eye,
twirl and whirl,
long looks up legs,
red lips—
wide eyes.

no names stitched
for recognition,
chromosome deficient—
just one organism
until determined
they are competition
in matching skirts.

PAINTED LEGS

it won't do,
grandmother said,
to show bare legs.
you need smoothness
and muscle tone—
not to mention the
barrier between
the hands of men
or even their eyes
and your flesh.

no silk to be had,
and there's a war,
by the way.
but, still—
the illusion must
remain intact,
nothing's changed!

a line painted straight,
help each other
out girls—
munitions by day,
eyebrow pencils
by night.
trade coveralls
for painted legs
and do right.

Rosie may be
a riveter,
but she's also
got to be riveting.
because those men,
they're coming back
and they'll expect
your stockinged legs
and painted smiles
to greet them.

grandmother says,
do your part,
but don't forget
your place,
and please,
just paint your legs.

UNMENTIONABLES

a girdle stripped
that i'd folded neat,
in a square,
with my panties underneath—
a secret in this place
where no secrets
could hide with
my back opened
by loose ties,
my spine shivering
its knobs against
cold paper as feet
slide into place
and you pull me
down in this
dingy room.
i turn my face to
see anything
beyond this belly—
still flat, underneath
a stained gown
worn by so many
desperations before me.
my underthings,
unmentionables,
slid to the floor
in a graceless puddle,
not arranged neatly
as i'd meant them to be—

but there they are,
just like he'd said,
looking better on the
floor at the edge of
his bed, that night
he entered me, then
left me cold
with a fistful
of dingy green paper
wadded into a pocketbook
handed over to this
man with a coat hanger
and eyes that look
defeated. and i wonder
if this will be
the last gown
i might ever wear.

PRETTY THING

magical myth sending
seed pearl steps
across a half lit stage,
toes pressed against
fabric and glue,
a body raised to
impossible heights,
matching the standards
she was born to—
aching bones and
blisters sheathed underneath
pink satin,
the same as the edge
of her first baby blanket,
slipped against a pain-free cheek,
cooed delighted darling.
she is felled,
a tree,
a willow,
into the waiting arms,
of a ballerino flattened to the stage—
standing strong
while she bleeds beauty
into a toe box,
because sometimes
(most times)
it hurts to be a pretty thing.

ANATOMY OF A DRESS

do not choose a neckline
too low— though we
call you sweetheart until
the time comes to grow
and bloom, swelling to show
decolletage, beckoning hands
or mouths that never noticed,
now itching to touch,
tongues seeking to slake.

be watchful of hemlines
that land a secret
code across:
ankles,
calves,
and—
"you asked for it" thighs,
alerted to all-seeing eyes.

even those sleeves,
baring shoulders—
much less wanton
than knees—
a litmus test,
your willingness
to undress,
to bare,
freckled skin
for the enjoyment of men.

zippered along a spine,
fit and flare calling
all entry points—
no twirl will defend.
best done—
trembling vertical,
blending into
brick
&
mortar,
for there is far less
molestation at the edges
of a life lived safely
out of bounds.

we are skirts of
signal flags—
calling to ships,
but boarded by pirates
in treacherous waters,
dragged under the power
of a full fathom five,
against clenched fists,
and hungry mouths.

treasure tossed,
without care.
unkind
&
unfair—
the fact still remains
this
is
the
anatomy of a dress.

PUBLICATIONS

My Hem and Silhouette Shame were first published in Mookychick October 2018.

S(mocked) and Painted Legs were first published in Burning House Press October 2018.

Dupioni Darkling was first published in You Are Not Your Rape (anthology-Rhythm and Bone Press) November 2018.

ACKNOWLEDGMENTS

The beginning of this book didn't actually begin with any writing at all. I'd like to thank the Art Students League of New York for their tireless effort in providing classes for all levels of artists. I was fortunate enough to paint in some of the same studios frequented by Jackson Pollock and Georgia O'Keeffe. The history of the space, along with their commitment to the artistic community and continuing education was a huge source of inspiration to me.

My ideas as a painter were fostered and cared for by the incredible instructor at the Art Students League of New York, Nicki Orbach, who taught me on a personalized level through her classes and friendship. Nicki braved incredible pain and a struggle with cancer to come to her students every day and put them first. She taught me to go with my gut and to do what feels right. She was my biggest supporter for my project "The Charles James Abstraction", which ultimately led to the poetry created in this book. Though she is no longer with us, I think of her often and certainly every time I see my paintings. Her legacy continues through me and countless other students she made a deep and lasting connection with.

Additionally, I'm grateful to The Metropolitan Museum of Art in New York City and the Rijksmuseum in Amsterdam for providing countless exhibits and programs that educate and inspire the general population. Without access to these thoughtfully curated exhibits I would not have had the opportunity to engage all of my senses. Thank you for all of the work you do in making art accessible for everyone.

I'd also like to thank Magda Knight, Tianna G. Hansen, Kristin Garth and the wonderful editors from She Speaks UK for publishing poems that appear in this book. A special thank you to Elisabeth Horan, who saw this manuscript in its earliest form and connected me with Mark Davidson of The Hedgehog Poetry Press. Without all this support, these poems may have stayed as files on my computer. I am thrilled to have them published and cared for and to be able to share my vision with the wider world.